THE M.G. RAMACHANDRAN

A BIOGRAPHY

R.SANTHOSH KRISHNAN

Copyright © R.santhosh Krishnan
All Rights Reserved.

This book has been published with all efforts taken to make the material error-free after the consent of the author. However, the author and the publisher do not assume and hereby disclaim any liability to any party for any loss, damage, or disruption caused by errors or omissions, whether such errors or omissions result from negligence, accident, or any other cause.

While every effort has been made to avoid any mistake or omission, this publication is being sold on the condition and understanding that neither the author nor the publishers or printers would be liable in any manner to any person by reason of any mistake or omission in this publication or for any action taken or omitted to be taken or advice rendered or accepted on the basis of this work. For any defect in printing or binding the publishers will be liable only to replace the defective copy by another copy of this work then available.

M.G.RAMACHANDRAN A BIOGRAPHY (1917- 1987) LIFE OF MGR Anna Dravinda Munnetra Kazhagam popularly known as the ADMK was started by M.G.RAMACHANDRAN whose original name was Maruthoor Gopal Ramachandran.he was born at kandi in srilanka on 17th january 1971 as the fifth child of Gopal Menon and Sathyabhama.Gopal menon started his career as a magistate and later he was professor.As he died in srilanka in 1919 sathyabhama,shifted to the family to kumbakonam.There her eleven year old daughter also died .thus sorrows and suffering tourned the family. M.G.R CAREER: MGR stared his education at alayadi school near kumbakonam in 1923.the poverty that his family suffered at the early stage didn't permit to continue his education third standard was educated.so his brother chakrapani joined the madurai original boys dramatic companyas an assistant actor for salary of five rupees per one month to be acompanied by his brother MGR.both the brother were fedup with the drama company and the chance for the act in cinema field. MGR ENTER INTO CINEMA WORLD: MGR entered into the cinema world field in 1934 that time MGR AGE was 40 enter into the cinema field.His first the role of the police inspector in the cinema "sathi leelavathi".Then he was elevated to the rank of the hero through the "Rajakumari"relesed in1947.subsequence the films "Abimanyu","mohini","Rajamukthi" relesed in 1948 and the "Rathna kumar" relesed in 1949 lifted his prestiage step by step.After that MGR acted in the film "marudhanttu illavarasi ".relesed in the 1950,which was scriped by the m.karunanidhi.during the shooting of this film the love blessomed between MGR and janagi took them to marriage later.In 1958,MGR directed "Nadoodi mannan" and the role took in it,helped him to reach the tamil cinema world. VARRIETY NAME OF MGR : MGR was admired for his qualities all over the world with titled by the MGR. • PURATCHI THALAIVAR • PURATCHI NADIGAR • MAKKAL NAYAGAN He presented the characters in a disciplaint form and the roll of an unconscious drunkard that he acted in his 100th films 'olivilakku' released in 1968 won for him mass administration. The fame MGR won in the cinema world is still a fresh in the minds of the people. The role of a poor man helping the poor that MGR acted in the cinema 'Mannathi Mannan' and his effective dialogues in 'nadoodi mannan' and 'Deiva thai' cinemas served as the flashbacks of the dravidian bravery. M.G.Ramchandran and DMK: MGR was equally popular both in cinema and politics which had been properly utilized by the dmk party for its development.however the then chiefminister karunanithi became jealous of his popularty and stared taking steps to discoular him.he encouraged his son M.K.MUTHU to involve in the cinema field in 1971.M.K.Muthu was directed to show his attention deeply in the cinema field and was encouraged to complete with MGR.So M.K.Muthu became an actor in the cinema field.due to there arose a dispute between the two fan club.karunanidhi went to the extent of writing scripts for his son M.K.Muthu's cinema.In fact copied the activity of MGR includes hair style.yet on his father could not succeed in reducing the popularty of MGR. Introduction of AIADMK: During the period of the Annathurai the DMK party was very clean but his demise led the party became corruptive.being very honest MGR opposed the party corruption and attacked karunanidhi for his neglect of Annathurai principles.Karunanidhi and some of his minister could not tolerate the aggressive attitude of MGR.they decided to take disciplinary action aganist him as directed by the executive council member of the DMK party.the executive meeting of DMK which was held on 10th october 1972 suspected MGR from the DMK party and party and asked the explanation. M.K.Karunanidhi,the president and nedunchezian,the General secretary of the DMK, announced the suspension of MGR from the party and got endorsed by 26 out of 31 members of the DMK executive. He was given a show cause notice on 11-10-1972 and asked to his suspension reached MGR at sathya studio. When he was in the midst of the shooting of a Tamil film entitled 'Netru Indru Naalai'. After Completing his shooting he met the press reporters. His fans got stunned on hearing the suspension of their hero from DMK party.The mediatory talks of Nanchil Manoharan and Mrs.Satyavani Muthu also failed. His treasurer post because of his insistence on the accounts of the amount collected for the party leaders because of his insistence on the accounts of the amount collected for the party conference at madurai in 1972. MGR guessed an amount of five lakhs of rupees collected for the purpose but Karunanidhi stood on only one lakh. At this hour of crisis the public consisting of peoples students, peasants and the workers stood with MGR. In the mean time Nanjil Manoharan, the jointSecretary of DMK party announced the removal of MGR from the party in a public meeting held at Thirukalankuntam in 1972. Hearing this news a rebellion took place at Madurai in favour of MGR. A majority of the youngsters of low class families participated in unlawful activites in favour of MGR. The protestors caused damages to the state owned transport buses to the tune of more than 60 lakhs. The fans of MGR ran through out the city streets attacked the DMK flags and the pictures of Karunanidhi. Violent incidents agitations and protests throughout Tamil Nadu paralaysed the DMK administration over a fortnight. But MGR instead of getting shocked or surprised with events was found in relaxed mood and smiling face.Despite these development karunanidhi was confident of the firmness of the DMK party.on 18 october 1972,MGR started a new political party known as 'Anna Dravida Munnetra Kazhagam'. The party adopted a flag 4 inches in length, 3 inches in breath, the upper half in red colour and the lower half in black with an emblem of Annathurai in the middle in the flag. On 23rd December 1972, MGR was given a public reception by a lakh of people at Kancheepuram. The MGR fan clubs and some DMK branches initially converted themselves into ADMK branches providing the frame work for the party organization. Some dissident DMK leaders who had lost factional battles joined the ADMK soon after its formation. Bulk of the student wing of the DMK like S.D.Somasundaram and azhagu Thirunavukarasu. At the beginning Vannai Mu. Pandian. H.V.Hande, a kannadika Brahmin who had been with the swantra party and G.R. Edmund, a christian from the fisher men caste became state level ADMK leaders.significition of female support for the ADMK was reflection in the existence of a strong women's wing to the party.political alignments follwed lines of stratifiction when the ADMK broadened its coalition after assuming power.unlike DMK the ADMK did not have a party organ periodical. However the newspaper "thennagam" published by some prominet defection from DMK was adopted as the party organ to be replaced by the Annathurai later.The Nadars and sc community hithero extended to the congress party was diverted towards the new party by P.H.Pandian.The local legislator for the local legislator for over a decade restrained the violence of some Mudhukulathor farmers and cattlerustlers. Further the initiation of many minor public works in the constituency helped the ADMK grow steadily during MGR's rules.The ADMK regime supported the growth of hindu revivalism which did not find a place in the DMK agenda and accepted Annaisms as the manifesto. M.R.Radha shot the MGR January of 1967 in madras was excitingly busy. The Madras Corporation was preparing to host a grand reception for noted singer M.S.Subbulakshmi who had just delivered a concert at the united nations. Political parties were stepping up campaigning for the impending elections, and cricket enthusiasts were seeking out tickets to watch the third test between west Indians and India. For fans of MGR, however, the release of his new film Thaiukku Thalaimagan was the most important event in the month. On january 12, they were getting ready to put up festoons and celebrate the release the following day. But things took a different turn that day.To their shock, agony and anger, MGR was shot by fellow actor M.R.Radha at the former's residence in Nandambakkam, st.Thomas Mount, around 5 p.m Many rushed to government Royappetah hospital where he was taken for emergency treatment. Chanting 'long live MGR',they pelted stones and went on a rampage that lasted till about 9 p.m. News spread that Radha, who shot MGR, had tried to commit suicide by shooting himself and was admitted to the same hospital for threatment.A group of MGR fans descended on Radha's house in st.Thomas Mount and vandalized the property. A prohibitory order was promulgated. Both the actors had to be shifted to government general hospital for surgery. The bullet that entered near MGR's left ear had 'lodged itself behind the first vertebra'. In the case of Radha, one bullet fired at the right temple 'had caused an injury and fractured the skull. Another fire in the neck got embedded at the rear part of the neck'. But it was impossible for any vechicle to plough through the crowd out side Royapettah GH. The police had to forcefully clear the way and by 10.15 p.m.,both the actors were moved to the GH in the same ambulance.Doctors removed the bullets from the Radha's body but in the case of MGR, they feared dislodging the bullet would cause further damage to the first cervical vertebra. They decided not to touch the bullet . Both actors gained conciousness by 11a.m. The following day. Anxious fans were on the edge through the night. Anxious well-wishers and fans welcomed news of the actors' well- being the next day.The shooting case was not as simple as it seemed. The investigation and lengthy trail that followed unfolded a complicated story.k.k.vasu,who was with Radha in MGR's house when the shooting took place,was the key withness.he was a film producer,and in 1966,had borrowed money from RADHA to produce a movie titled petraltham pillaya with MGR in the lead. The movie did well and vasu repaid the loan with interest.In january 1967,Radha approched vasu to produce another film with MGR in the lead again.On the morning of january 12,both met to discuss the project. By 4.30 that evening,both reached MGR's house in Nandambakkam. They were seated in the reception hall.Radha placed the leather bag he was carrying on the table and waited for MGR to show. The story is clear up this point and all the parties boardly agreed with the narration. But the account began to vary here on. As vasu and MGR recalled in court ,when they were discussing the detail of the proposted movie,Radha stood up. MGR asked Radha to be seated, but he did not heed the words.MGR and vasu continuedtalking when all of sudden they heard a loud noise. MGR felt a shooting pain and covered his palm to feel blood ooze out. He looked up and saw Radha standing with a revolver in his hand. Radha stepped back, shot himself in the right temple, and then in the neck. MGR managed to walk to the portico and asked his driver to take him to the hospital. Radha, however, had a different story. According to him, when MGR met them in the reception hall, the matinee idol scolded Radha for writing negative articles about him. "Brother,you are writing articles saying that I am conspiring saying to kill Mr.kamaraj (then Cheif Minister of tamil nadu). Thereafter you are threatening to shoot.It does not preent me from talking on the same lines",MGR allegedly said. But Radha denied it.Even as they were engaged in a heated argument,Radha heard a loud noise felt giddy.He realized he had been shot in the temple and saw MGR pointing a gun at him. Radha claimbed that,as a relex,he rushed toward MGR,snatched the gun and fired a shot in return. Radha was in hosipital until january 30.After that he was in A-class prison of madras central jail. The Election campaign was in full swing by then and the iconic picture of MGR sitting on a hosipital bed with a heavily bandaged neck was widely circulated. Election results were announced on february 23 and DMK trounced congress to form a new government.MGR defeated his congress rival by an impressive margin. On february 27,the police filed a chargesheet accusing Radha of a murder attempt on MGR,and a suicide bid.the police also said Radha owned the revolver used in the shooting.its licence had expired in 1964. Annaism: MGR gave a clear explanation for Annaism. According to him Annaism is synthesis of the good matters and principles filtered from Gandhianisms,communism and capitalism. It aimed at the establishment of a casteless and classless society through democraptic stuggles.Settlements of communal and linguistic disputes through peaceful means formed the policy and principles of ADMK. Karunanidhi was shocked to see the growth of the new party in the initial stage,he constituted an enquiry committee against MGR. He appointed a retired judge of the chengalpet session court namely justice S.vengadesan in 1972 to enquie ADMK party men and give the report for all the complaints relation to the ADMK party men. It was a mile stone in the history of tamilnadu politics. ATTROCITIES AT SALEM: In Salem district, a DMK meeting took place on 29-1-1972 at paramathi vellore. The meeting took place at kanthaswamy gounder high school. As the students of that school opposed it. Kanthswamy gounder High school.As the student of that school opposed it.karunanidhi's police crushed the student with iron hands.Teacher of the school were attacked by the police officials. Hearing this incident the salem district INTUC president Ramamurthy and the secretary Kalyanasundaram submitted a petition to the governer. On 12-1-1974, another such incident took place at kumarapalayam in salem. In a factory a factory a women named Fathima was raped by four DMK party functionaries. But by the influennce of the DMK leaders a case was registered under section 302 of IPC againt fathima's husband and he was imprisoned. On 24-6- 1974 the ADMK supporters but no action was taken by the DMK chief. A Harijan women kamalammal was raped by six DMK men at Mathanoor, a place in north Arcot district. But no action was taken. Due to the initative steps taken by Maragadam Chandrasekhar some action was taken for name sake. MGR'S Education reforms TN's tech base: Policies of his govt Replacing PUC, Establishment pvt Engineering colleges helped to Achieve Excellence, says former minister MGR's rule is often seen as a time of expansion in welfare but industrial and economic stagnation. Experts point to a robust industrial foundation being laid during the Congress rule followed by the late 1990s and then onwards when investment picked up in the state. But MGR's education minister C Aranganayagam disputes the idea and says that the reforms MGR executed helped to created a large pool of skilled, technical manpower thet is today among the positives for the state as an investment destination. Aranganayagam points to two specific policy initiative of MGR; abolition of pre-university course (PUC) in favour of higher secondary education in schools and the starting of private engineering colleges. When the question arose whether to conduct class 11 and class 12 in school or colleges, MGR apparently asked Aranganayag am, "What would be more beneficial to the poor in the villages ?" Aranganayagam told him the poor would benefit if higher secondary education was offered in the same schools so that rural students would not have to travel far. There were less than 200 colleges compared to the more than 5,000 schools in the state at that time. Bureaucrats argued that schools lacked the infrastructure and did noy even have science labs to support higher secondary education. MGR set up labs in every school at a cost of about Rs 1 lakh each and higher secondary education began in 1978. Class 12 pass rates were in range of 90% wheres PUC pass rates were typically 40%. has To MGR,this was a great social leveler as many lower class student were become commpetitive and most of them who had failed PUC were now on equal terms with the privilged class.Only 80,000 student used to take the PUC exam,but nearly 9 lakh student took the class 12 board this year. But the quality of education deteriorated since higher education was started in school,says career consulting jayaprakash gandhi."The vision of the MGR government has been undermined by succcessivee government, as a result of which the standard of education has lowered. Nearly one tenth of the students writing board exam today are centum scorers,but they struggle,but they struggle to cope in their first"engineering futher adds that a compromise was made when PUC was made abolished in therms of qualified teacher,and infrastructure. Te transition in the higher secondary education meant college had to be steamlined. With more student passing out of schools by 1980,the state had a shortage of colleges.There were only six government engineering college in the state. The government did not have the funds to start colleges and so MGR appealed to private parties. KCG vergshree came to forword to set up the Hindustan college of engineering that later became Hindustan University.MGR's education reforms, as many of his other intitiatives,political as well as social sides too. Aranganayagam believed that the new insititution should focus to uplift four main caste groups in the state - nadar,gounders,mukkulathors and vanniyars. "I strongly belived that TN could not advance without the progress of its caste groups. We invitied s jagathraksha kan and G viswanathan to starts colleges for the benefits of the vanniyar community.soon after,we gave licences to jeppiar and AC shanmugam ." says Aranganayagam. Sixteen college oftechnical education were started in 1983.MGR ensured a lion's share for the poor by ruling that 50% of the seats in private institution will be filled by the government."We did not allow the college management to charge capitation fee,but they did it behind closed doors,demanding Rs 40,000 to 50,000 for a seat. Today they charge much more,"says Aranganayam. Add to that,the engineering colleges are not in tandem with advancements in the industry. Gandhi says "Engineering college must reinvast at least 20% of their earning to improve infrastructure. But not many do it". Today ,there are more than 2.5 lakh seats in engineering colleges,of which about 40% remain vacant. Many argue thre are too many engineering chasing too few jobs whereas there is death of trained technicians. This issue to was on MGR mind. " MGR did have a vision for vocationalosation as an alternative to higher secondary education with an arrangement where these students could join engineering college later. But college heads and bureaucrats did not cooperate. Schemes in the Educational work: Inorder to provide pride to tamil as the official language of the state the AIADMK revived the poet Lauret-Ship in the Government of Tamil Nadu. Further the Government ordered the implementation of certain reforms in Tamil language introduced by E.V.R.Periyar. A separate Tamil university at Tanjore was also set up in 1981. lastly the AIADMK was instrumental in conduction the grand world Fifth Tamil Conference during january 4-10- 1981 at madurai. The setting up of Bharathiyar University at truchi, The Tamil university at coimbatore, The Anna university of technology at madras were the great contributions of MGR's regime. The setting up of women 's univerity at kodaikanal and the Alagappa university at karaikudi, increasing the emphasis on Tamil medium courses,granting of autonomous status to several college,giving emphasis on correspondence education and more attention to non formal and non formal and adult education wereso carried out during his tenure as chief minister of tamil nadu .these were some of structural adminstration improvements achived in the field of education under AIADMK. The AIADMK's attiude toward hindu revivalism did not charge much after MGR's death. These shift in the ADMK's choice of allies were kept with ADMK to forge links with whichever party appeared stronger in national politics. The ADMK regime redistributed property and changed the profile of income distribution less than the DMK regime did. DINDIGUL BYE-

ELECTION: On 20-5-1973 the bye election to the Dindigul parliamentary constituency came due to the death of Rajangam in 1971.In this election candidates of DMK,ADMK and congress parties contested. Finally the ADMK candidate mayathevar won the election.The Dindigul bye election marked a turning point in the politics of tamilnadu for ADMK party. Similar election held for the coimbatore constituency and pondicherry constituency were also won by the ADMK candidates.It gave a boost to the ADMK party members. During the DMK regime there was internal disorder in tamil nadu. So the opposition party got a chance to fame corruptive charges against the DMK. SCHEMES OF MGR: MGR gradually dominated the tamil nadu poltics and arranged his party in an organized manner.By launching mid day meal scheme he enjoyed the continued support of the electorate.In views of giving a national outlook to the his party itwas renamed as AIADMK on 12-9- 1976. Krishna water project ,mid day metal scheme, tanjavur tamil university are the living monuments of the MGR government. The AIADMK government allotted eight lakhs rupees for procuring and displaying framed picture framed picture of MGR eating with poor children in every one of the noon metal centres. Earlier it was the film magazines such as cinema kadir and Gundoosi which published MGR donation periodically. AIADMK government under MGR taxed the rich agitator Rajendran to keep statue for him. By the nutritious meal scheme MGR told that he could see GOD in the laughing faces of the poor people. Even though the people of Tamilnadu gave a warm welcome to then prime minister Indira Gandhi they gave the votes for the MGR. After the dismissal of the MGR government by Indira Gandhi MGR won the next election. The victory which he got was remarkable . In USA, the world famous university like visconsin, chicago,bergli and california invited MGR to give lectures. Even through MGR acted in one cinema a year, the ran for several days. In

1982,MGR introduced jayalalitha as the frontline leader in his party. He also appointed her as the propoganda secretary for the AIADMK party. A notice was published in the name ofwith powers to ban films which had been certified by the central board of film certification. The bill was provoked by the succes of a film was NEETHIKKU THANDANAI scriped by karunandhi. The film was as one would as one would expect quite critical of MGR rule. 1977-A BLOW TO D.M.K: The year 1977 witnessed a total changes in the politics of tamil nadu. In India the long hegemony of the congress was brought to an abrupt which came into existence just on the eve of the 1977 elections. In Tamil nadu, M.G.RAMACHANDRAN a film actor turned poltical who had founded a new political party, scored a spectacularelectroal victory and capturned power with in five year after founding the party . Both these phenomena were interesting and sensational events in the annals of political development of the country. His convincing triumphs of the dindigul bye-election and the parliament election were clean indication of his ascending politics supremacy. HELPING HAND OF MGR: MGR was a symbol of hope for the poor in Tamil Nadu. Having no children of his own he adopted the poor as his successors. Almost on every occasion, he donated money for the benefits of the poor. In his later cinemas, he appered with young heroines such as jayalalitha,latha and manjula,and in a number of cinemas he acted with more than one heroine. There are a number of MGR fan,association in different parts of tamil nadu named as "thrice born MGR fans association". He was invariably garlanded with unimaginably huge garlands localy known a 'Dindu malai' Which had later acquired a new name 'MGR maalai' made of at least ten thousand roses. Both in real life and on screen, MGR was represented as one among the common people and at the same time he was distinct form and stood above them.An AIADMK MLA, tamarai kani from srivilliputhoor constructed a small shrine for his leader outside his house and people offered prayers there . As soon as he died, one of his close association and beneficiary of his rule jeppiyar announced that he was planning to construct a temple for MGR . In remembrance of that he started a university in the name of MGR's mother named as sathyabhama deemed university. MGR's charisma took him to unprecedented heights and he won the assebly election of 1977, 1980 and 1984. M.G.RAMACHANDRAN AS Chief-minister of Tamil nadu: Once he became chief-minister of tamil nadu, he placed great emphasis on social development, especially education. One of his most successful policies was the conservation of the "Midday Meal scheme",introduction by the popular congress chief minister and king maker K.Kamaraj iyya, which already was encouraging underprivileged children to attend school, into "MGR 's nutritious meal schemes" in the government-run and aided schools in Tamil nadu by adding saththurundai — a nutritious sugary flour dumpling. This scheme was at a cost of RS.1 billion and was imposed in 1982. A little more than 120,000 children of the state were benifited. He Also introduced women's special buses. He introduced a liquor ban in the state and preservation of old temple and historical monument, ultimately increasing the state's tourist income. He set up a free school for the cinema technicians children in kodambakkam called MGR primary & Higher secondary school which provided free mid day meals in the 1950. he led the ADMK to victory in 1984 assembly election,despite not taking part in the campaigning. At that time he was under going medical treatment in America and his images were boardcast in tamil nadu through cinema halls. This was an effective campaign tactic and ADMK won the election claiming around 56% of assembly seat, indicating the depth of his popular support. He won his seat in double landslide victory in 1984. he still holds the record of being the chief-minister with the higest consistent longevity of more than a decade. Karunanidhi claimed on 1 april 2009 and again on13 may 2012 that MGR was ready for the merger of his party with DMK in 1979, with Biju patnaik acting as the meditor. The plan failed because panruti ramchandran, who was close to MGR acted in as spoiled and MGR changed the mind. DEATH OF M.G.RAMACHANDRAN: In october 1984,MGR was diagnosed with kidney failure as a result of diabetes, which was soon follwed by a mild attack and massive stroke. He was rushed to the downstate medical centre in new york city, united states for treatment undergoing a kidney transplant. Despite his poor health, he did contest the assembly election hield later that year while still confined to the hospital, winning from andipatti. During the election, photo of a MGR recuperating in hospital were published,created a sympathy wave among the people. MGR returned to madras on february 1985 following his recovery. He was sworn in as chief-minister of tamil nadu for the trird consecutive team on 10 february 1985. the next two year and 10 months were spent in frequeent trips to the united states for treatment. MGR never fully recovered from his multiple health problem and died on 24 december 1987 at 3:30 AM in his ramavaram gardens residence in manapakkam after his prolongen illness. He was 70 years old, just a month away before his 7 1 st brithday. His death sparked offa frenzy of looting and rioting all over the state. Shops, cinemas,buses and other public and private property became the target of violence let loose. The police to resort issuing shoot at sight order. Schools and college immediately announced holidays till the situation came under control. Violence during the funeral alone left 29 people dead and police personnel badly wounded. His remains were buried in the northern end of marina beach is now MGR memorial which is adjacent to the anna memorial near in the MGR memorial. State of affairs continued for almost a month across Tamil Nadu. Around one million people allowed his remain around 30 followers commited to suicide and people and people had their heads tonsured. After his death, his political party, all india anna dhravinda munnetra kazhagam, split between his wife jannaki ramachandran and j.jayalalitha they merged 1989. In 1989 Dr.M.G.R. Home and higher secondary school for the speech and hearing impaired was established at the erswhile residence MGR Garden, Ramavaram, in Accordance with his last will & treatment written january 1987. his official residence at 27, arcot street, t.nagar is now MGR memborial house and is open for public viewing. His film studio, sathya studios, has been converted into a women's college. BHARAT RATNA AWARD TO MGR: After hi death in 1987, he became the thrid chief-minister from the state of Tamil Nadu to receive the bharat ratna after C.Rajagopalchariand and k.kamaraj iyya. The timing of the award was controversial, due to the fact that it was given so quickly after his death and he was elected as chief-minister only 11 year before the award. Many opponents, mostly out side Tamil Nadu, criticised then ruling party INC, under rajiv gandhi to have influnced the selection committee to give the award to help win the uupcoming 1989 Lok sabha election. The ruling party formation a coalition with j.jayalalitha,the succesors to MGR at that time, were able to sweep Tamil Nadu, winning 38 out of 39 seats, INC were however unable to win nationally. To commemorate MGR's Birth in 2017, the ministry of finance,Government of India decided to issue 100 and 5 coins that would bears his image as a portrait along with an inscription of "Dr.M.G. Ramachandran Birth centenary. MGR IN TAMIL NADU LEGISLATIVE ASSEMBLY year constituency result position party Fro m to 1967 st.thomas mout won Member of legislative DMK 19/ 03/ 04/01/ 71 67 1971 st.thomas mout won Member of legislative DMK 15/ 03/ 71 31/01/ 76 1977 Aruppukottai won chief-minister AIAD MK 30/ 06/ 77 17/02/ 80 1980 Madurai West won chief-minister AIAD MK 09/ 06/ 80 15/11/ 84 1984 Andipatti won chief-minister AIAD MK 10/ 02/ 85 24/12/ 87 AWARD TO CINEMA FILED TO THE MGR:

year Event/ venue Award Work to filed 1974 The world university (arizona) university of Madras Honoring doctorate For the contributions to indian cinema , for the contributions to cinema 1988 Government of india Bharat Rathna For the contributions to arts CINEMA FIELD AWARD TO MGR year Event Award category Film /work 1965 Film fare award south Special jury award Enga veettu pillai 1968 Tamil nadu state film award Best actor,best film Kudiyirundha koyil 1969 Film fare award south Best film Adimaippen 1971 National Film Award Best actor Rickshawkaran MGR AS PRODUCER AND DIRECTOR IN FILED: • 1958 – NADODI MANNAN , PRODUCER AND DIRECTOR • 1969- ADIMAI PENN , PRODUCER • 1973- ULLAGAM SUTRUM VALIBAN , PRODUCER AND DIRECTOR • 1977- MADHURAIYAI METTA SUNDHARAPANDIYAN, DIRECTOR MGR PHOTO INFORMATION THIS PICTURE IS MGR AND HIS WIFE JANNAKI 2.THIS PICTURE WAS MGR AND HIS FAN AND PEOPLE 3.THIS PICTURE IS MGR SMILE IN SPEECH 4.THIS PICTURE IS MGR DEATH 5.THIS PICTURE WAS MGR POSTED PLACE 6.THIS PICTURE WAS MGR MEMORIAL HOUSE. ABOUT OF AUTHOR: R.SANTHOSH KRISHNAN S/O RADHA KRISHNAN I AM STUDYING IN SCHOOL MY AGE IS :13 MY ADDRESS:4/94 PONNIYAMMAN KOVIL STREET,KARASANGAL,PADAPPAI-601301 CHENNAI. SUPPORT HELPING HAND OF ME • MY FAMILY MEMBER • MY SISTER:LAVANYA AND JEEVITHA • MY UNCLE SON:PRASATH • MOST WISHES TO MY BLESS GODM.G.RAMACHANDRAN A BIOGRAPHY (1917- 1987) LIFE OF MGR Anna Dravinda Munnetra Kazhagam popularly known as the ADMK was started by M.G.RAMACHANDRAN whose original name was Maruthoor Gopal Ramachandran.he was born at kandi in srilanka on 17th january 1971 as the fifth child of Gopal Menon and Sathyabhama.Gopal menon started his career as a magistate and later he was professor.As he died in srilanka in 1919 sathyabhama,shifted to the family to kumbakonam.There her eleven year old daughter also died .thus sorrows and suffering tourned the family. M.G.R CAREER: MGR stared his education at alayadi school near kumbakonam in 1923.the poverty that his family suffered at the early stage didn't permit to continue his education third standard was educated.so his brother chakrapani joined the madurai original boys dramatic companyas an assistant actor for salary of five rupees per one month to be acompanied by his brother MGR.both the brother were fedup with the drama company and the chance for the act in cinema field. MGR ENTER INTO CINEMA WORLD: MGR entered into the cinema world field in 1934 that time MGR AGE was 40 enter into the cinema field.His first the role of the police inspector in the cinema "sathi leelavathi".Then he was elevated to the rank of the hero through the "Rajakumari"relesed in1947.subsequence the films "Abimanyu","mohini","Rajamukthi" relesed in 1948 and the "Rathna kumar" relesed in 1949 lifted his prestiage step by step.After that MGR acted in the film "marudhanttu illavarasi ".relesed in the 1950,which was scriped by the m.karunanidhi.during the shooting of this film the love blessomed between MGR and janagi took them to marriage later.In 1958,MGR directed "Nadoodi mannan" and the role took in it,helped him to reach the tamil cinema world. VARRIETY NAME OF MGR : MGR was admired for his qualities all over the world with titled by the MGR. • PURATCHI THALAIVAR • PURATCHI NADIGAR • MAKKAL NAYAGAN He presented the characters in a disciplaint form and the roll of an unconscious drunkard that he acted in his 100th films 'olivilakku' released in 1968 won for him mass administration. The fame MGR won in the cinema world is still a fresh in the minds of the people. The role of a poor man helping the poor that MGR acted in the cinema 'Mannathi Mannan' and his effective dialogues in 'nadoodi mannan' and 'Deiva thai' cinemas served as the flashbacks of the dravidian bravery. M.G.Ramchandran and DMK:

MGR was equally popular both in cinema and politics which had been properly utilized by the dmk party for its development.however the then chiefminister karunanithi became jealous of his popularty and stared taking steps to discoular him.he encouraged his son M.K.MUTHU to involve in the cinema field in 1971.M.K.Muthu was directed to show his attention deeply in the cinema field and was encouraged to complete with MGR.So M.K.Muthu became an actor in the cinema field.due to there arose a dispute between the two fan club.karunanidhi went to the extent of writing scripts for his son M.K.Muthu's cinema.In fact copied the activity of MGR includes hair style.yet on his father could not succeed in reducing the popularty of MGR. Introduction of AIADMK: During the period of the Annathurai the DMK party was very clean but his demise led the party became corruptive.being very honest MGR opposed the party corruption and attacked karunanidhi for his neglect of Annathurai principles.Karunanidhi and some of his minister could not tolerate the aggressive attitude of MGR.they decided to take disciplinary action aganist him as directed by the executive council member of the DMK party.the executive meeting of DMK which was held on 10th october 1972 suspected MGR from the DMK party and party and asked the explanation. M.K.Karunanidhi,the president and nedunchezian,the General secretary of the DMK, announced the suspension of MGR from the party and got endorsed by 26 out of 31 members of the DMK executive. He was given a show cause notice on 11-10-1972 and asked to his suspension reached MGR at sathya studio. When he was in the midst of the shooting of a Tamil film entitled 'Netru Indru Naalai'. After Completing his shooting he met the press reporters. His fans got stunned on hearing the suspension of their hero from DMK party.The mediatory talks of Nanchil Manoharan and Mrs.Satyavani Muthu also failed. His treasurer post because of his insistence on the accounts of the amount collected for the party leaders because of his insistence on the accounts of the amount collected for the party conference at madurai in 1972. MGR guessed an amount of five lakhs of rupees collected for the purpose but Karunanidhi stood on only one lakh. At this hour of crisis the public consisting of peoples students, peasants and the workers stood with MGR. In the mean time Nanjil Manoharan, the jointSecretary of DMK party announced the removal of MGR from the party in a public meeting held at Thirukalankuntam in 1972. Hearing this news a rebellion took place at Madurai in favour of MGR. A majority of the youngsters of low class families participated in unlawful activites in favour of MGR. The protestors caused damages to the state owned transport buses to the tune of more than 60 lakhs. The fans of MGR ran through out the city streets attacked the DMK flags and the pictures of Karunanidhi. Violent incidents agitations and protests throughout Tamil Nadu paralaysed the DMK administration over a fortnight. But MGR instead of getting shocked or surprised with events was found in relaxed mood and smiling face.Despite these development karunanidhi was confident of the firmness of the DMK party.on 18 october 1972,MGR started a new political party known as 'Anna Dravida Munnetra Kazhagam'. The party adopted a flag 4 inches in length, 3 inches in breath, the upper half in red colour and the lower half in black with an emblem of Annathurai in the middle in the flag. On 23rd December 1972, MGR was given a public reception by a lakh of people at Kancheepuram. The MGR fan clubs and some DMK branches initially converted themselves into ADMK branches providing the frame work for the party organization. Some dissident DMK leaders who had lost factional battles joined the ADMK soon after its formation. Bulk of the student wing of the DMK like S.D.Somasundaram and azhagu Thirunavukarasu. At the beginning Vannai Mu. Pandian. H.V.Hande, a kannadika Brahmin who had been with the swantra party and G.R. Edmund, a christian from the fisher men caste became state level ADMK leaders.significition of female support for the ADMK was reflection in the existence of a strong women's wing to the party.political alignments follwed lines of stratifiction when the ADMK broadened its coalition after assuming power.unlike DMK the ADMK did not have a party organ periodical. However the newspaper "thennagam" published by some prominet defection from DMK was adopted as the party organ to be replaced by the Annathurai later.The Nadars and sc community hithero extended to the congress party was diverted towards the new party by P.H.Pandian.The local legislator for the local legislator for over a decade restrained the violence of some Mudhukulathor farmers and cattlerustlers. Further the initiation of many minor public works in the constituency helped the ADMK grow steadily during MGR's rules.The ADMK regime supported the growth of hindu revivalism which did not find a place in the DMK agenda and accepted Annaisms as the manifesto. M.R.Radha shot the MGR January of 1967 in madras was excitingly busy. The Madras Corporation was preparing to host a grand reception for noted singer M.S.Subbulakshmi who had just delivered a concert at the united nations. Political parties were stepping up campaigning for the impending elections, and cricket enthusiasts were seeking out tickets to watch the third test between west Indians and India. For fans of MGR, however, the release of his new film Thaiukku Thalaimagan was the most important event in the month. On january 12, they were getting ready to put up festoons and celebrate the release the following day. But things took a different turn that day.To their shock, agony and anger, MGR was shot by fellow actor M.R.Radha at the former's residence in Nandambakkam, st.Thomas Mount, around 5 p.m Many rushed to government Royappetah hospital where he was taken for emergency treatment. Chanting 'long live MGR',they pelted stones and went on a rampage that lasted till about 9 p.m. News spread that Radha, who shot MGR, had tried to commit suicide by shooting himself and was admitted to the same hospital for threatment.A group of MGR fans descended on Radha's house in st.Thomas Mount and vandalized the property. A prohibitory order was promulgated. Both the actors had to be shifted to government general hospital for surgery. The bullet that entered near MGR's left ear had 'lodged itself behind the first vertebra'. In the case of Radha, one bullet fired at the right temple 'had caused an injury and fractured the skull. Another fire in the neck got embedded at the rear part of the neck'. But it was impossible for any vechicle to plough through the crowd out side Royapettah GH. The police had to forcefully clear the way and by 10.15 p.m.,both the actors were moved to the GH in the same ambulance.Doctors removed the bullets from the Radha's body but in the case of MGR, they feared dislodging the bullet would cause further damage to the first cervical vertebra. They decided not to touch the bullet . Both actors gained conciousness by 11a.m. The following day. Anxious fans were on the edge through the night. Anxious well-wishers and fans welcomed news of the actors' well- being the next day.The shooting case was not as simple as it seemed. The investigation and lengthy trail that followed unfolded a complicated story.k.k.vasu,who was with Radha in MGR's house when the shooting took place,was the key withness.he was a film producer,and in 1966,had borrowed money from RADHA to produce a movie titled petraltham pillaya with MGR in the lead. The movie did well and vasu repaid the loan with interest.In january 1967,Radha approched vasu to produce another film with MGR in the lead again.On the morning of january 12,both met to discuss the project. By 4.30 that evening,both reached MGR's house in Nandambakkam. They were seated in the reception hall.Radha placed the leather bag he was carrying on the table and waited for MGR to show. The story is clear up this point and all the parties boardly agreed with the narration. But the account began to vary here on. As vasu and MGR recalled in court ,when they were discussing the detail of the proposted movie,Radha stood up. MGR asked Radha to be seated, but he did not heed the words.MGR and vasu continuedtalking when all of sudden they heard a loud noise. MGR felt a shooting pain and covered his palm to feel blood ooze out. He looked up and saw Radha standing with a revolver in his hand. Radha stepped back, shot himself in the right temple, and then in the neck. MGR managed to walk to the portico and asked his driver to take him to the hospital. Radha, however, had a different story. According to him, when MGR met them in the reception hall, the matinee idol scolded Radha for writing negative articles about him. "Brother,you are writing articles saying that I am conspiring saying to kill Mr.kamaraj (then Cheif Minister of tamil nadu). Thereafter you are threatening to shoot.It does not preent me from talking on the same lines",MGR allegedly said. But Radha denied it.Even as they were engaged in a heated argument,Radha heard a loud noise felt giddy.He realized he had been shot in the temple and saw MGR pointing a gun at him. Radha claimbed that,as a relex,he rushed toward MGR,snatched the gun and fired a shot in return. Radha was in hosipital until january 30.After that he was in A-class prison of madras central jail. The Election campaign was in full swing by then and the iconic picture of MGR sitting on a hosipital bed with a heavily bandaged neck was widely circulated. Election results were announced on february 23 and DMK trounced congress to form a new government.MGR defeated his congress rival by an impressive margin. On february 27,the police filed a chargesheet accusing Radha of a murder attempt on MGR,and a suicide bid.the police also said Radha owned the revolver used in the shooting.its licence had expired in 1964. Annaism: MGR gave a clear explanation for Annaism. According to him Annaism is synthesis of the good matters and principles filtered from Gandhianisms,communism and capitalism. It aimed at the establishment of a casteless and classless society through democraptic stuggles.Settlements of communal and linguistic disputes through peaceful means formed the policy and principles of ADMK. Karunanidhi was shocked to see the growth of the new party in the initial stage,he constituted an enquiry committee against MGR. He appointed a retired judge of the chengalpet session court namely justice S.vengadesan in 1972 to enquie ADMK party men and give the report for all the complaints relation to the ADMK party men. It was a mile stone in the history of tamilnadu politics. ATTROCITIES AT SALEM: In Salem district, a DMK meeting took place on 29-1-1972 at paramathi vellore. The meeting took place at kanthaswamy gounder high school. As the students of that school opposed it. Kanthswamy gounder High school.As the student of that school opposed it.karunanidhi's police crushed the student with iron hands.Teacher of the school were attacked by the police officials. Hearing this incident the salem district INTUC president Ramamurthy and the secretary Kalyanasundaram submitted a petition to the governer. On 12-1-1974, another such incident took place at kumarapalayam in salem. In a factory a factory a women named Fathima was raped by four DMK party functionaries. But by the influennce of the DMK leaders a case was registered under section 302 of IPC againt fathima's husband and he was imprisoned. On 24-6- 1974 the ADMK supporters but no action was taken by the DMK chief. A Harijan women kamalammal was raped by six DMK men at Mathanoor, a place in north Arcot district. But no action was taken. Due to the initative steps taken by Maragadam Chandrasekhar some action was taken for name sake. MGR'S Education reforms TN's tech base: Policies of his govt Replacing PUC, Establishment pvt Engineering colleges helped to Achieve Excellence, says former minister MGR's rule is often seen as a time of expansion in welfare but industrial and economic stagnation. Experts point to a robust industrial foundation being laid during the Congress rule followed by the late 1990s and then onwards when investment picked up in the state. But MGR's education minister C Aranganayagam disputes the idea and says that the reforms MGR executed helped to created a large pool of skilled, technical manpower thet is today among the positives for the state as an investment destination. Aranganayagam points to two specific policy initiative of MGR; abolition of pre-university course (PUC) in favour of higher secondary education in schools and the starting of private engineering colleges. When the question arose whether to conduct class 11 and class 12 in school or colleges, MGR apparently asked Aranganayag am, "What would be more beneficial to the poor in the villages ?" Aranganayagam told him the poor would benefit if higher secondary education was offered in the same schools so that rural students would not have to travel far. There were less than 200 colleges compared to the more than 5,000 schools in the state at that time. Bureaucrats argued that schools lacked the infrastructure and did noy even have science labs to support higher secondary education. MGR set up labs in every school at a cost of about Rs 1 lakh each and higher secondary education began in 1978. Class 12 pass rates were in range of 90% wheres PUC pass rates were typically 40%. has To MGR,this was a great social leveler as many lower class student were become commpetitive and most of them who had failed PUC were now on equal terms with the privilged class.Only 80,000 student used to take the PUC exam,but nearly 9 lakh student took the class 12 board this year. But the quality of education deteriorated since higher education was started in school,says career consulting jayaprakash gandhi."The vision of the MGR government has been undermined by succcessivee government, as a result of which the standard of education has lowered. Nearly one tenth of the students writing board exam today are centum scorers,but they struggle,but they struggle to cope in their first"engineering futher adds that a compromise was made when PUC was made abolished in therms of qualified teacher,and infrastructure. Te transition in the higher secondary education meant college had to be steamlined. With more student passing out of schools by 1980,the state had a shortage of colleges.There were only six government engineering college in the state. The government did not have the funds to start colleges and so MGR appealed to private parties. KCG vergshree came to forword to set up the Hindustan college of engineering that later became Hindustan University.MGR's education reforms, as many of his other intitiatives,political as well as social sides too. Aranganayagam believed that the new insititution should focus to uplift four main caste groups in the state - nadar,gounders,mukkulathors and vanniyars. "I strongly belived that TN could not advance without the progress of its caste groups. We invitied s jagathraksha kan and G viswanathan to starts colleges for the benefits of the vanniyar community.soon after,we gave licences to jeppiar and AC shanmugam ." says Aranganayagam. Sixteen college oftechnical education were started in 1983.MGR ensured a lion's share for the poor by ruling that 50% of the seats in private institution will be filled by the government."We did not allow the college management to charge capitation fee,but they did it behind closed doors,demanding Rs 40,000 to 50,000 for a seat. Today they charge much more,"says Aranganayam. Add to that,the engineering colleges are not in tandem with advancements in the industry. Gandhi says "Engineering college must reinvast at least 20% of their earning to improve infrastructure. But not many do it". Today ,there are more than 2.5 lakh seats in engineering colleges,of which about 40% remain vacant. Many argue thre are too many engineering chasing too few jobs whereas there is death of trained technicians. This issue to was on MGR mind. " MGR did have a vision for vocationalosation as an alternative to higher secondary education with an arrangement where these students could join engineering college later. But college heads and bureaucrats did not cooperate. Schemes in the Educational work: Inorder to provide pride to tamil as the official language of the state the AIADMK revived the poet Lauret-Ship in the Government of Tamil Nadu. Further the Government ordered the implementation of certain reforms in Tamil language introduced by E.V.R.Periyar. A separate Tamil university at Tanjore was also set up in 1981. lastly the AIADMK was instrumental in conduction the grand world Fifth Tamil Conference during january 4-10- 1981 at madurai. The setting up of Bharathiyar University at truchi, The Tamil university at coimbatore, The Anna university of technology at madras were the great contributions of MGR's regime. The setting up of women 's univerity at kodaikanal and the Alagappa university at karaikudi, increasing the emphasis on Tamil medium courses,granting of autonomous status to several college,giving emphasis on correspondence education and more attention to non formal and non formal and adult education wereso carried out during his tenure as chief minister of tamil nadu .these were some of structural adminstration improvements achived in the field of education under AIADMK. The AIADMK's attiude toward hindu revivalism did not charge much after MGR's death. These shift in the ADMK's choice of allies were kept with ADMK to forge links with whichever party appeared stronger in national politics. The ADMK regime redistributed property and changed the profile of income distribution less than the DMK regime did. DINDIGUL BYE-ELECTION: On 20-5-1973 the bye election to the Dindigul parliamentary constituency came due to the death of Rajangam in 1971.In this election candidates of DMK,ADMK and congress parties contested. Finally the ADMK candidate mayathevar won the election.The Dindigul bye election marked a turning point in the politics of tamilnadu for ADMK party. Similar election held for the coimbatore constituency and pondicherry constituency were also won by the ADMK candidates.It gave a boost to the ADMK party members. During the DMK regime there was internal disorder in tamil nadu. So the opposition party got a chance to fame corruptive charges against the DMK. SCHEMES OF MGR: MGR gradually dominated the tamil nadu poltics and arranged his party in an organized manner.By launching mid day meal scheme he enjoyed the continued support of the electorate.In views of giving a national outlook to the his party itwas renamed as AIADMK on 12-9- 1976. Krishna water project ,mid day metal scheme, tanjavur tamil university are the living monuments of the MGR government. The AIADMK government allotted eight lakhs rupees for procuring and displaying framed picture framed picture of MGR eating with poor children in every one of the noon metal centres. Earlier it was the film magazines such as cinema kadir and Gundoosi which published MGR donation periodically. AIADMK government under MGR taxed the rich agitator Rajendran to keep statue for him. By the nutritious meal scheme MGR told that he could see GOD in the laughing faces of the poor people. Even though the people of Tamilnadu gave a warm welcome to then prime minister Indira Gandhi they gave the votes for the MGR. After the dismissal of the MGR government by Indira Gandhi MGR won the next election. The victory which he got was remarkable . In USA, the world famous university like visconsin, chicago,bergli and california invited MGR to give lectures. Even through MGR acted in one cinema a year, the ran for several days. In 1982,MGR introduced jayalalitha as the frontline leader in his party. He also appointed her as the propoganda secretary for the AIADMK party. A notice was published in the name ofwith powers to ban films which had been certified by the central board of film certification. The bill was provoked by the succes of a film was NEETHIKKU THANDANAI scriped by karunandhi. The film was as one would as one would expect quite critical of MGR rule. 1977-A BLOW TO D.M.K:

The year 1977 witnessed a total changes in the politics of tamil nadu. In India the long hegemony of the congress was brought to an abrupt which came into existence just on the eve of the 1977 elections. In Tamil nadu, M.G.RAMACHANDRAN a film actor turned poltical who had founded a new political party, scored a spectacularelectroal victory and capturned power with in five year after founding the party . Both these phenomena were interesting and sensational events in the annals of political development of the country. His convincing triumphs of the dindigul bye-election and the parliament election were clean indication of his ascending politics supremacy. HELPING HAND OF MGR: MGR was a symbol of hope for the poor in Tamil Nadu. Having no children of his own he adopted the poor as his successors. Almost on every occasion, he donated money for the benefits of the poor. In his later cinemas, he appered with young heroines such as jayalalitha,latha and manjula,and in a number of cinemas he acted with more than one heroine. There are a number of MGR fan,association in different parts of tamil nadu named as "thrice born MGR fans association". He was invariably garlanded with unimaginably huge garlands localy known a 'Dindu malai' Which had later acquired a new name 'MGR maalai' made of at least ten thousand roses. Both in real life and on screen, MGR was represented as one among the common people and at the same time he was distinct form and stood above them.An AIADMK MLA, tamarai kani from srivilliputhoor constructed a small shrine for his leader outside his house and people offered prayers there . As soon as he died, one of his close association and beneficiary of his rule jeppiyar announced that he was planning to construct a temple for MGR . In remembrance of that he started a university in the name of MGR's mother named as sathyabhama deemed university. MGR's charisma took him to unprecedented heights and he won the assebly election of 1977, 1980 and 1984. M.G.RAMACHANDRAN AS Chief-minister of

Tamil nadu: Once he became chief-minister of tamil nadu, he placed great emphasis on social development, especially education. One of his most successful policies was the conservation of the "Midday Meal scheme",introduction by the popular congress chief minister and king maker K.Kamaraj iyya, which already was encouraging underprivileged children to attend school, into "MGR 's nutritious meal schemes" in the government-run and aided schools in Tamil nadu by adding saththurundai – a nutritious sugary flour dumpling. This scheme was at a cost of RS.1 billion and was imposed in 1982. A little more than 120,000 children of the state were benifited. He Also introduced women's special buses. He introduced a liquor ban in the state and preservation of old temple and historical monument, ultimately increasing the state's tourist income. He set up a free school for the cinema technicians children in kodambakkam called MGR primary & Higher secondary school which provided free mid day meals in the 1950. he led the ADMK to victory in 1984 assembly election,despite not taking part in the campaigning. At that time he was under going medical treatment in America and his images were boardcast in tamil nadu through cinema halls. This was an effective campaign tactic and ADMK won the election claiming around 56% of assembly seat, indicating the depth of his popular support. He won his seat in double landslide victory in 1984. he still holds the record of being the chief-minister with the higest consistent longevity of more than a decade. Karunanidhi claimed on 1 april 2009 and again on13 may 2012 that MGR was ready for the merger of his party with DMK in 1979, with Biju patnaik acting as the meditor. The plan failed because panruti ramchandran, who was close to MGR acted in as spoiled and MGR changed the mind. DEATH OF M.G.RAMACHANDRAN: In october 1984,MGR was diagnosed with kidney failure as a result of diabetes, which was soon follwed by a mild attack and massive stroke. He was rushed to the downstate medical centre in new york city, united states for treatment undergoing a kidney transplant. Despite his poor health, he did contest the assembly election hield later that year while still confined to the hospital, winning from andipatti. During the election, photo of a MGR recuperating in hospital were published,created a sympathy wave among the people. MGR returned to madras on february 1985 following his recovery. He was sworn in as chief-minister of tamil nadu for the trird consecutive team on 10 february 1985. the next two year and 10 months were spent in frequeent trips to the united states for treatment. MGR never fully recovered from his multiple health problem and died on 24 december 1987 at 3:30 AM in his ramavaram gardens residence in manapakkam after his prolongen illness. He was 70 years old, just a month away before his 7 1 st brithday. His death sparked offa frenzy of looting and rioting all over the state. Shops, cinemas,buses and other public and private property became the target of violence let loose. The police to resort issuing shoot at sight order. Schools and college immediately announced holidays till the situation came under control. Violence during the funeral alone left 29 people dead and police personnel badly wounded. His remains were buried in the northern end of marina beach is now MGR memorial which is adjacent to the anna memorial near in the MGR memorial. State of affairs continued for almost a month across Tamil Nadu. Around one million people allowed his remain around 30 followers commited to suicide and people and people had their heads tonsured. After his death, his political party, all india anna dhravinda munnetra kazhagam, split between his wife jannaki ramachandran and j.jayalalitha they merged 1989. In 1989 Dr.M.G.R. Home and higher secondary school for the speech and hearing impaired was established at the erswhile residence MGR Garden, Ramavaram, in Accordance with his last will & treatment written january 1987. his official residence at 27, arcot street, t.nagar is now MGR memborial house and is open for public viewing. His film studio, sathya studios, has been converted into a women's college. BHARAT RATNA AWARD TO MGR: After hi death in 1987, he became the thrid chief-minister from the state of Tamil Nadu to receive the bharat ratna after C.Rajagopalchariand and k.kamaraj iyya. The timing of the award was controversial, due to the fact that it was given so quickly after his death and he was elected as chief-minister only 11 year before the award. Many opponents, mostly out side Tamil Nadu, criticised then ruling party INC, under rajiv gandhi to have influnced the selection committee to give the award to help win the uupcoming 1989 Lok sabha election. The ruling party formation a coalition with j.jayalalitha,the succesors to MGR at that time, were able to sweep Tamil Nadu, winning 38 out of 39 seats, INC were however unable to win nationally. To commemorate MGR's Birth in 2017, the ministry of finance,Government of India decided to issue 100 and 5 coins that would bears his image as a portrait along with an inscription of "Dr.M.G. Ramachandran Birth centenary. MGR IN TAMIL NADU LEGISLATIVE ASSEMBLY year constituency result position party From to 1967 st.thomas mout won Member of legislative DMK 19/ 03/ 04/01/ 71 67 1971 st.thomas mout won Member of legislative DMK 15/ 03/ 71 31/01/ 76 1977 Aruppukottai won chief-minister AIAD MK 30/ 06/ 77 17/02/ 80 1980 Madurai West won chief-minister AIAD MK 09/ 06/ 80 15/11/ 84 1984 Andipatti won chief-minister AIAD MK 10/ 02/ 85 24/12/ 87 AWARD TO CINEMA FILED TO THE MGR: year Event/ venue Award Work to filed 1974 The world university (arizona) university of Madras Honoring doctorate For the contributions to indian cinema , for the contributions to cinema 1988 Government of india Bharat Rathna For the contributions to arts CINEMA FIELD AWARD TO MGR year Event Award category Film /work 1965 Film fare award south Special jury award Enga veettu pillai 1968 Tamil nadu state film award Best actor,best film

Kudiyirundha koyil 1969 Film fare award south Best film Adimaippen 1971 National Film Award Best actor Rickshawkaran MGR AS PRODUCER AND DIRECTOR IN FILED: • 1958 — NADODI MANNAN , PRODUCER AND DIRECTOR • 1969- ADIMAI PENN , PRODUCER • 1973- ULLAGAM SUTRUM VALIBAN , PRODUCER AND DIRECTOR • 1977- MADHURAIYAI METTA SUNDHARAPANDIYAN, DIRECTOR MGR PHOTO INFORMATION THIS PICTURE IS MGR AND HIS WIFE JANNAKI 2.THIS PICTURE WAS MGR AND HIS FAN AND PEOPLE 3.THIS PICTURE IS MGR SMILE IN SPEECH 4.THIS PICTURE IS MGR DEATH 5.THIS PICTURE WAS MGR POSTED PLACE 6.THIS PICTURE WAS MGR MEMORIAL HOUSE. ABOUT OF AUTHOR: R.SANTHOSH KRISHNAN S/O RADHA KRISHNAN I AM STUDYING IN SCHOOL MY AGE IS :13 MY ADDRESS:4/94 PONNIYAMMAN KOVIL STREET,KARASANGAL,PADAPPAI-601301 CHENNAI. SUPPORT HELPING HAND OF ME • MY FAMILY MEMBER • MY SISTER:LAVANYA AND JEEVITHA • MY UNCLE SON:PRASATH • MOST WISHES TO MY BLESS GOD

Contents

www.ingramcontent.com/pod-product-compliance
Lightning Source LLC
Chambersburg PA
CBHW031435250726
48656CB00002B/1003